CONSENSUS THROUGH CONVERSATION

D0043907

CONSENSUS THROUGH CONVERSATION

How to Achieve High-Commitment Decisions

by
Larry Dressler

BERRETT-KOEHLER PUBLISHERS, INC.
San Francisco

Berrett-Koehler Publishers, Inc.
235 Montgomery Street, Suite 650
San Francisco, CA 94104-2916
Tel: (415) 288-0260   Fax: (415) 362-2512   www.bkconnection.com

Ordering Information
Quantity sales. Special discounts are available on quantity purchases by corporations, associations, and others. For details, contact the "Special Sales Department" at the Berrett-Koehler address above.

Individual sales. Berrett-Koehler publications are available through most bookstores. They can also be ordered direct from Berrett-Koehler:
Tel: (800) 929-2929; Fax: (802) 864-7626; www.bkconnection.com

Orders for college textbook/course adoption use. Please contact Berrett-Koehler:
Tel: (800) 929-2929; Fax: (802) 864-7626.

Orders by U.S. trade bookstores and wholesalers. Please contact Publishers Group West, 1700 Fourth Street, Berkeley, CA 94710. Tel: (510) 528-1444; Fax (510) 528-3444.

Berrett-Koehler and the BK logo are registered trademarks of Berrett-Koehler Publishers, Inc.

Printed in the United States of America

Berrett-Koehler books are printed on long-lasting acid-paper. When it is available, we choose paper that has been manufactured by environmentally responsible processes. These may include using trees grown in sustainable forests, incorporating recycled paper, minimizing chlorine in bleaching, or recycling the energy produced at the paper mill.

Library of Congress Cataloging-in-Publication Data

Dressler, Larry, 1961-
   Consensus through conversation : how to achieve high-commitment decisions / by Larry Dressler.
      p. cm.
   Includes index.
   ISBN-10: 1-57675-419-7 (pbk.)
   ISBN-13: 978-1-57675-419-1 (pbk.)
   1. Group decision-making.   2. Consensus (Social sciences)   I. Title.
HD30.23.D737 2006
658.4'036—dc22

                                                    2006012020

First Edition
11   10   09   08   07   06   10   9   8   7   6   5   4   3   2   1

To my parents, Harold and Selma Dressler, who have taught me about the joy of animated conversation (especially at the dinner table), the potential for one person to make a difference in the world, and the possibilities created when people come together to act on what matters to them.

Contents

KEY TO THE ICONS

Throughout the *Consensus Pocket Guide* you will find different icons. These are quick examples, resources, and tools that may be particularly useful to you. Graphic icons help you to search out this information quickly.

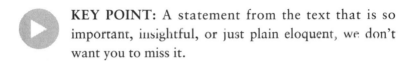 **KEY POINT:** A statement from the text that is so important, insightful, or just plain eloquent, we don't want you to miss it.

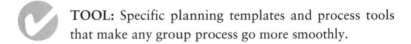 **TOOL:** Specific planning templates and process tools that make any group process go more smoothly.

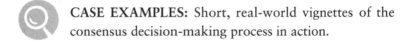 **CASE EXAMPLES:** Short, real-world vignettes of the consensus decision-making process in action.

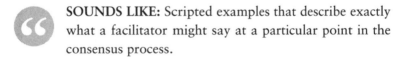 **SOUNDS LIKE:** Scripted examples that describe exactly what a facilitator might say at a particular point in the consensus process.

BY PIERRE GAGNON
Former CEO, Mitsubishi Motors
of North America

My years at Saturn and Mitsubishi taught me that inclusive leadership is one of the most powerful tools in business today. The command and control model of management is now obsolete. In today's complex business environment, there has never been a greater need for including others in critical decisions. Yet, I have found very few business leaders who are comfortable with the notion of deciding by consensus. They feel they are giving up power and prestige. Having used the consensus approach for more than a decade, I strongly believe that consensus decision making yields higher-quality and higher-commitment decisions. It is not, however, a process that is easily implemented. To make it work, a leader must have a deep-rooted, fundamental belief that broader participation in decision making yields much higher-quality decisions and incredibly faster execution. I was fortunate to learn the process at Saturn, but truly experienced the unbelievable power of consensus at Mitsubishi.

When I arrived at Mitsubishi in April 1997, I found a fragmented company with an unclear brand identity, disappointing product quality, and an adversarial relationship with dealers. It's no wonder the company had lost money for ten consecutive years in North America. I was informed a month after joining the company that the Japanese parent company was seriously considering pulling out of America. Needless to say, I felt an enormous sense of urgency to change the business fundamentals of the U.S.-based company. We immediately formed twelve change teams to tackle the critical areas of the business, from product quality to brand development. I urgently needed to fully leverage the talents of the best and brightest in the organization. I needed to make them part of the solution, not part of the problem. I needed their buy-in in order to execute faster. We were running out of time. That's when I was introduced to Larry Dressler. The author was tireless and relentless in helping us implement a consensus decision-making process.

Our first session with the Regional Marketing Council took 36 hours to reach consensus on a dramatically new direction. Larry was masterful in facilitating the entire session. Somehow he was able to extract the best ideas and inspire everyone to seek the best possible outcome for the company. He uncovered hidden agendas, crafted proposals, and led us to consensus. A high level of commitment ensued, and the rest is history. Looking back, it was our toughest session in the entire change process.

Larry subsequently implemented the consensus decision model in all twelve change teams and the newly formed National Dealer Advisory Board. It was amazing to see the process work. By putting the right people in the room to have the right conversations and to go beyond agreeing-to actually commit together-we experienced the power of consensus building. Mitsubishi Motors' North American operations subsequently flourished with five consecutive record years of profits, increasing revenue by 94 percent and establishing all-time sales and market share records. We went from making decisions in a vacuum and operating in silos to a company that was unified, aligned, effective, and profitable.

Consensus Through Conversation: How to Achieve High-Commitment Decisions was written by an author who has real-life experience in planning and implementing a consensus decision-making process at a major automotive company and in many other diverse settings. Not only does Larry Dressler fully understand the concept, he knows what it takes to implement the process in a real-world situation. The author offers a comprehensive, step-by-step process to effectively implement consensus decision making in your organization.

If you're looking for higher-quality decisions, increased trust, faster execution, and higher commitment, then this process is for you. It's my hope that in reading this book, you go beyond creating more effective meetings and better deliberation through more meaningful conversation. I hope you use the principles and practices described in this book to fundamentally change the culture in your organization or community. It will set you apart from the pack.

PREFACE

If you are a consultant, manager, meeting facilitator, team leader, community organizer, or simply someone who is involved in lots of group decisions, *Consensus Through Conversation* was written for you.

I wrote the book based on a number of important premises. First, consensus is a misunderstood, underused, and at times misused method for inclusive decision-making. Second, consensus is most effective when every participant understands the fundamental principles and practices. Third, building consensus in groups involves a learnable set of ideas and skills that do not require a week-long workshop to master. Fourth and perhaps most importantly, consensus building is not a skill reserved for top leaders and professionals. By definition, consensus is for everyone and can be learned by anyone.

Consensus Through Conversation is a portable, easy-to-read reference to help you facilitate and participate in consensus decision-making processes. It contains the basic principles and methods for making consensus work, whether in the corporate boardroom or in the community meeting hall. This book was developed as a companion to *Consensus Cards*™, a tool I developed to assist groups in making consensus-based decisions. The book can be used on its own or in conjunction with this tool.

This is not a general guide to effective meeting facilitation. It is written for people who are taking part in a specific kind of meeting—one in which a consensus decision must be made. While implementing the tips and methods described in this book will no doubt improve most meetings, my focus is to help you create effective *consensus* decision-making processes. If you are looking for more general references on how to conduct better meetings, you will find some of my favorites in the Resources Guide in the final section of this book.

Consensus can be a powerful and transformative tool. However, it is by no means a panacea that will transform your organization into a perfectly democratic or otherwise utopian world. Your job as a leader will be to decide when and where to use a consensus-based approach (see Guidelines on page 4).

As an organizational change consultant, I often learn as much from my clients as I teach them. The person who taught me the most about what consensus actually looks like in action is auto industry executive Pierre Gagnon. As Pierre describes in the Foreword, he brought consensus-based decision-making from Saturn Motors to Mitsubishi where he served as that company's CEO. Pierre doesn't just use consensus as a tool, he leads from the fundamental belief that participation yields higher-quality, higher-commitment decisions.

For me, *doing* the work of consensus building is quite a bit easier than writing about it. My secret to writing was to surround myself with people who are clear thinkers, painfully honest givers of feedback, and skillful writers. For their good counsel and collaboration, I want to acknowledge with gratitude Angela Antenore, Tree Bressen, Mary Campbell, Sherri Cannon, Jane Haubrich Casperson, Marcia Daszko, Susan Ferguson, Katrina Harms, Sandy Heierbacher, Diana Ho, Peggy Holman, Brian Ondre, Diane Robbins, Arnie Rubin, Hal Scogin, Kathe Sweeney, Annie Tornick, Johanna Vondeling, and Melissa Weiss. Whether facing the daunting task of writing or the sometimes exhausting work of helping groups reach consensus, at the end of the day, I get to come home to my wife, Linda Smith, who is my most solid sounding board, supporter, and inspiration. To all these people, thank you! Your thumbprints are all over this book.

My career has been dedicated to helping people have conversations that result in high-quality decisions, increased trust, higher commitment, and real learning. In my experience, the proper use of consensus fosters these outcomes. As you read this book, I hope you will begin to recognize more opportunities for using the tools of consensus in your organization and community.

Larry Dressler
Boulder, Colorado
July 2006

The New Rules
of Decision-Making

*You think that because you understand ONE, you
understand TWO because one and one make two.
But you must understand AND.*

—Sufi Proverb

For today's leaders, understanding *AND* means discovering the
power of putting the right people in the same room at the right
moment for the right conversation. Understanding *AND* means
recognizing that there are times when you gain influence, credibility and commitment by including others in critical decisions.
Understanding *AND* means embracing the idea that multiple,
often conflicting perspectives can be creatively combined into
breakthrough solutions.

AND is about inclusive leadership—the art of bringing diverse voices to the table and seeing what can be learned and accomplished. In the past, a more inclusive way of leading and making decisions was a philosophical choice. Today, it is a business imperative. In every corner of organizational life, collective decision-making has become the rule rather than the exception. Let's look at some of the reasons why this is becoming truer each day.

- Hierarchical organizations are giving way to flat networks. The "leader as brain, employees as body" model of organizations is obsolete. Leaders recognize that in today's complex and changing environment, one person rarely has a corner on the knowledge and judgment market.

- Technology has put information in the hands of the people who need it most—particularly those on the front lines. Well-informed decisions must include the perspective of those with first-hand experience.

- The issues organizations and communities face are increasingly complex. The only way to navigate complexity is to test the implications and impacts of our solutions by drawing on a wide range of resources and perspectives. When we fail to involve the right stakeholders, we often create problems that are more significant than the original problem we were trying to address.

- A new generation of knowledge workers are voting with their feet. They want to be included. They want to influence decisions that impact their work. If they can't, they take their skills and knowledge and go elsewhere.

- The ability to *implement* a decision quickly is as important as agility in *making* the decision. Fast implementation is determined by the extent to which people understand and support the decision. Participation accelerates execution.

Given the foregoing trends, consensus has become a more and more common approach to decision-making in organizations. As you move toward more inclusive leadership, consensus is one of those strategic tools that you will want to have in your repertoire.

What Is Consensus?

For the past fifteen years, most of my work as a consultant has been based on a single premise:

> *Real change does not come from decree, pressure, permission, or persuasion. It comes from people who are passionately and personally committed to a decision or direction they have helped to shape.*

If you want to turn your organization's bystanders or cynics into owners, give them a meaningful voice in decisions that impact their work. When people are invited to come together to share their ideas, concerns, and needs, they become engaged. They move from being passive recipients of instructions to committed champions of decisions. This is the power of deciding together.

Consensus Defined

Consensus is a cooperative process in which all group members develop and agree to support a decision that is in the best interest of the whole. In consensus, the input of every member is carefully considered and there is a good faith effort to address all legitimate concerns.

Consensus has been achieved when every person involved in the decision can say: "I believe this is the best decision we can arrive at for the organization at this time, and I will support its implementation."

What makes consensus such a powerful tool? Simply *agreeing* with a proposal is not true consensus. Consensus implies *commitment* to a decision. When group members commit to a decision, they oblige themselves to do their part in putting that decision into action.

Consensus is also a process of *discovery* in which people attempt to combine the collective wisdom of all participants into the best possible decision.

Consensus is not just another decision-making approach. It is not a unanimous decision in which all group members' personal preferences are satisfied. Consensus is also not a majority vote in which some larger segment of the group gets to make the decision. Majority voting casts some individuals as "winners" and others as "losers." In consensus everyone wins because shared interests are served.

Finally, consensus is not a coercive or manipulative tactic to get members to conform to some preordained decision. The goal of consensus is not to *appear* participative. It is to *be* participative. When members submit to pressures or authority without really agreeing with a decision, the result is "false consensus" that ultimately leads to resentment, cynicism, and inaction.

Beliefs That Guide Consensus

Like any decision-making method, consensus is based on a number of important beliefs. Before using consensus, you must ask yourself and group members, "Are these beliefs consistent with who we are or who we aspire to be as an organization?"

There are four basic beliefs that guide any consensus-building process.

Cooperative Search for Solutions

Consensus is a collaborative search for *common ground solutions* rather than a competitive effort to convince others to adopt a particular position. This requires that group members feel committed to a common purpose. Group members must be willing to give up "ownership" of their ideas and allow those ideas to be refined as concerns and alternative perspectives are put on the table. Consensus groups are at their best when individual participants can state their perspectives effectively while not jealously guarding their position as the "only right solution."

Disagreement as a Positive Force

Constructive, respectful disagreement is actively encouraged. Participants are expected to express different points of view, criticize ideas, and voice legitimate concerns to strengthen a proposal. In consensus, we use the tension created by our differences to move toward creative solutions—not toward compromise or mediocrity.

Every Voice Matters

Consensus seeks to balance power differences. Because consensus requires the support of every group member, individuals have a great deal of influence over decisions, regardless of their status or authority in the group.

> In consensus, it is the responsibility of the group to make sure legitimate questions, concerns, and ideas get expressed and are fully considered, regardless of the source.

Decisions in the Interest of the Group

With influence comes responsibility. In consensus, decision makers agree to put aside their personal preferences to support the group's purpose, values, and goals. Individual concerns, preferences, and values can and should enter into the discourse, but in the end the decision must serve the collective interests.

It is possible for an individual group member to disagree with a particular decision but consent to support it because:

- The group made a good faith effort to address all concerns raised.
- The decision serves the group's current purpose, values, and interests.
- The decision is one the individual can live with, though not his or her first choice.

Choosing the Right Decision-Making Approach

Using consensus for a particular decision is both a philosophical and pragmatic choice, generally made by formal leaders. Some leaders believe it is possible and desirable to use consensus for every decision (e.g., "we are a consensus organization").

I believe that the appropriateness of consensus as a decision method is situational. Consensus is most successful when certain conditions are present. As a leader or facilitator of the decision process, it is your job to evaluate whether the right combination of conditions exists to support the approach.

Consensus may be the **most logical** and **sensible** approach when:

- This is a high-stakes decision that, if made poorly, has the potential to fragment your team, project, department, organization, or community.
- A solution will be impossible to implement without strong support and cooperation from those who must implement it.

- No single individual in your organization or group possesses the authority to make the decision.
- No single individual in your organization or group possesses the knowledge required to make the decision.
- Constituents with a stake in the decision have very different perspectives that need to be brought together.
- A creative, multidisciplinary solution is needed to address a complex problem.

On the flip side, consensus may **not** be the most logical approach when:

- The decision is a *fait accompli*—that is, it has already been made, but there is a desire to create the appearance of participation.
- Making the decision quickly is more important than including broad-based information and mobilizing support for implementation.
- Individuals or groups who are essential to the quality of the decision or the credibility of the decision-making process are not available or refuse to participate.
- The decision is simply not important enough to warrant the time and energy a consensus process involves.

Alternatives to Consensus

If your goal is to involve stakeholders in a decision, consensus is not the only approach available. Let's take a quick look at some other ways to make decisions in groups.

To help illustrate each of these approaches, here is a familiar scenario.

My wife, Linda, and I are going out to dinner with two other couples on Saturday evening. We all have idiosyncrasies and special needs with regard to what we will eat. We share a common purpose, which is to spend the evening together over an enjoyable meal.

Unanimous Voting

Every member of the group, without exception, gets his or her "first choice." In other words, every member's individual preferences are met.

I suggest the local sushi restaurant, and every one of the other five people say sushi was their first choice as well. Everyone wins!

Pros: When individual members' interests match up perfectly with shared interests, there is no down side. Every member's needs get fully met, and therefore, every member is likely to feel completely committed to the decision.

Cons: Achieving true unanimity is a difficult, if not impossible, outcome to achieve for most decisions.

Majority Voting

Group members agree to adopt whatever decision most people (or some determined threshold percentage of the group) want to support.

When asked, four of the six friends want to eat Chinese food and two prefer Mexican food. The outvoted minority agrees to eat at the Chinese restaurant. I don't enjoy Chinese food but a vote's a vote. Plus, we need to make it to an 8:00 P.M. movie, so we don't have a lot of time to stand around and discuss where to eat.

Pros: Majority voting is particularly useful when the pressures to make a speedy decision outweigh the need to address all concerns or get full buy-in. A critical mass of support for some decisions is often adequate to ensure effective implementation.

Cons: The minority group often feels "robbed" and as a result, not highly committed to the final decision, especially if that same group finds itself frequently on the losing end of the vote. When this dynamic is set into motion, organizations run the risk of becoming fragmented because decisions lack support from an important, often vocal constituency.

At best, majority decisions produce the likelihood of creating some subgroup of uncommitted followers. At worst, these decisions can result in active resistance and even sabotage.

Some groups use majority voting as a back-up method in case consensus cannot be reached. I caution leaders against this because it undermines the spirit of consensus and reduces members' motivation to work toward common ground solutions (e.g., "If I hold a majority position, why should I work toward consensus if I know that the decision will eventually revert to a vote that I will win?").

Compromise

Each group member gives up an important interest in order to reach a decision that *partially* meets everyone's needs. When compromise is used, nobody gets their first choice but everyone gets some of their needs met.

Three group members want Chinese food, one wants Middle Eastern food, and two prefer Mexican food. We decide to go to the Food Court at the local shopping mall. Everyone gets to eat their food preference, but nobody is satisfied with the flavor or the atmosphere.

Pros: Compromise can be more efficient than consensus. Every member gets some of what is needed and is willing to trade off other, less-important concerns or needs.

Cons: Compromise focuses on trade-offs rather than a creative search for some "third way" to meet the whole group's needs and concerns. Usually, nobody gets what they really want.

Deferring to an Individual Leader or Expert

An authorized group member makes a final decision either with or without consultation from others who have a stake in the decision. This method is sometimes used as a back-up approach if consensus cannot be reached.

Since it is Jim's birthday this week, we are letting him choose the restaurant. He takes a quick poll of the group, gets feedback on some ideas he has, and decides we are going to the local French restaurant.

Pros: An individual decision-making approach can be more efficient than consensus because the final decision involves fewer people. Deferring to an individual is particularly appropriate when the need for quick and decisive action overrides any desire for idea exploration or group buy-in. Using an expert authority is useful when there is a lack of experience or knowledge of the issue in your organization and the group is willing to defer to a knowledgeable individual. Finally, this approach can be used effectively on issues for which there are several good alternative solutions, all of which would be acceptable.

Cons: Individual decision makers may fail to consult with stakeholders who have relevant knowledge and ideas. They may miss out on important information that would create a better decision and more effective implementation. With hierarchical decisions, there is also a risk that people will not feel a sense of ownership of the solution they are charged with implementing.

Consensus
How might the restaurant decision be addressed through a consensus-based approach? Here is one possible scenario:

Four of the friends say they would like to eat Thai food. We discuss this preference and discover that they enjoy spicy food with curry. But my wife, Linda, is severely allergic to peanuts, and Thai restaurants tend to have a lot of peanuts in the kitchen. This is too risky for us. Someone suggests the local Korean BBQ restaurant, but Melissa rejects the idea. We ask her about her concerns and she states that she is a vegetarian. Jim suggests a new vegetarian Indian restaurant in town. This meets the needs of our "spicy curry friends" and also addresses both Linda's and Melissa's concerns.

Pros: Consensus most often produces high levels of commitment and accelerated implementation because most critical obstacles have been anticipated and all key stakeholders are on board.

Cons: The actual decision may take a bit longer to make, particularly when there are strongly held perspectives and group members are less experienced in using the method.

Common Misconceptions

Before they had a direct experience with consensus, many of my clients, especially corporations, were resistant to using this approach. They were worried about bogging down decisions that needed to be made quickly. They were also concerned that if consensus was used for some decisions, employees would expect to have a voice in *every* decision. Misconceptions about consensus abound, particularly in the world of business. Let's take a more systematic look at some common fears people have about consensus.

Consensus Takes Too Much Time

Speed is often an important factor in decision-making. In considering the issue of time, be sure to ask yourself whether you actually need to decide quickly *or* implement quickly.

> A speedy decision made by an individual or through majority voting may be efficient, but it may also result in slower implementation due to resistance or unanticipated consequences. Many leaders who have used consensus would say, "Whatever time we lost during our decision-making phase, we gained in the implementation phase."

There is no denying that consensus can take more time than other decision processes, but it does not need to be a burdensome process. With practice a well-planned process and skillful facilitation groups can move toward consensus decisions relatively quickly.

Solutions Will Become Watered Down

One concern about consensus is that resulting decisions are mediocre or uninspired because they have become watered down by compromises necessary to secure the support of every group member. An effective consensus process does not compromise on core criteria for decisions. It seeks to find solutions that fully achieve the group's criteria and goals while at the same time addressing individual members' concerns.

Individuals with Personal Agendas Will Hijack the Process

In any group process there is a possibility that a dysfunctional member or outside agitator may derail the decision process. Preestablished ground rules, strong facilitation, and a clear distinction between legitimate and nonlegitimate "blocks" of a decision are essential to prevent this from happening. As you will learn in later chapters, effective consensus processes offer people ways to "stand aside" when they have concerns but do not feel the need to hold up the decision.

Managers and Formal Leaders Will Lose Their Authority

Managers are often concerned that agreeing to a consensus process means they are giving up their ability to influence the final decision. They wonder, "Am I abdicating my role as a leader if I use consensus?" There is a difference between laissez-faire leadership, which often looks like abdication, and participative leadership, which requires the leader's full engagement. In consensus formal leaders are equal members of the decision group. Like any other member, they can stop a proposal if they do not feel comfortable with the solution. An alternative model using consensus involves the appropriate group of stakeholders making a consensus-based recommendation to management for final approval.

"Shared Ownership" Results in No Accountability

The concern is that no one will take responsibility for implementing a consensus-based decision because it is a group decision, not a personal decision. However, no group member is anonymous or invisible in consensus—quite the contrary. True consensus requires every participant to proclaim publicly not just his or her agreement with a proposal but full "ownership" of the decision.

Consensus in Action

Consensus can be used in a variety of environments and situations. The diversity of groups that can benefit from consensus is remarkable. Quakers have used consensus as a way of making decisions for more than three centuries. A wide range of organizations have adopted and modified consensus as a means of arriving at unified decisions, including contemporary organizations like Saturn Motor Corporation, the U.S. Army, and Levi Strauss & Co. Here are some real-life examples of consensus in action. These examples demonstrate that consensus can be effective in large companies, not-for-profit organizations, government agencies, and grassroots community meetings.

CREATING A STRATEGIC VISION

A leading toy maker brings together leaders from its offices in Los Angeles and Hong Kong to devise a long-range vision for success in a rapidly changing industry. There are no obvious paths toward the vision. The CEO is looking for the group's best thinking. The new vision will require significant changes in nearly every part of the company, along with a high level of commitment from the leaders in the room. The group uses consensus to make sure that all perspectives are heard and to confirm commitment from each team member.

DECIDING AS A BOARD

A member-owned, cooperatively run grocery store is governed by a board of directors. Members of the board, along with its subcommittees, are elected to represent different constituencies, including shoppers, employees, and store managers. To make policy and merchandising decisions that reflect the entire membership, these governing groups use consensus-based decision making. Consensus enables the co-op market to arrive at creative decisions that simultaneously satisfy financial, customer service, environmental, and social responsibility interests.

MOBILIZING SUPPORT FOR ORGANIZATIONAL CHANGE

A multinational automobile maker establishes twelve different cross-functional teams assigned to revitalize key areas of the company, ranging from brand identity to manufacturing quality. Teams include high-level executives, dealership owners, and frontline staff from throughout the company. Each group works with an outside facilitator to formulate recommendations to the National Advisory Board, which consists of company executives and franchise owners. Consensus-based recommendations result in swift approval and rapid implementation.

DEVELOPING PUBLIC POLICY

A governor formed a special task force charged with recommending a comprehensive housing strategy for the state's farm workers. Members of the task force included representatives of farmers, farm laborers, housing developers, and various government agencies. Several of these constituencies had a long history of conflict, but they came together because this was a unique opportunity to obtain significant funding from the legislature. The legislature made it clear that a recommendation supported by all of the constituencies would carry more weight than competing proposals from the various special interest groups. The consensus process not only enabled a solution that took into account the many important perspectives in the room, but also went a long way toward building trust among the various stakeholder representatives.

As you can see from these examples, consensus can succeed in diverse settings and situations. A crucial step in all these cases is careful consideration that consensus is the best way to make the decision. Let's move on now to the other building blocks that lay the groundwork for effective decision-making by consensus.

How Do I Prepare?

When it comes to group decision-making, so much of what determines success occurs before anyone steps into the meeting room. The eight building blocks described in this chapter make up the foundation for a successful consensus process. They are:

- Determine whether consensus is a good fit
- Decide who to involve in the decision
- Enlist a skilled facilitator
- Clarify the group's scope and authority
- Educate group members
- Develop an agenda
- Gather the relevant information
- Start the meeting off right

Determine Whether Consensus Is a Good Fit

Consensus is a vehicle for getting to a particular destination. In this case, that destination is a high-quality decision to which key stakeholders are committed. Selecting the right vehicle to get you to your destination has a lot to do with the terrain. In the case of decision-making, the terrain is mostly characterized by shared beliefs of the group and willingness of formal power holders.

How do you determine whether consensus is the right method for your decision process? First, go back to the two lists for determining when consensus does and does not make sense in the section "Choosing the Right Decision-Making Approach" on page 6. Second, assess the group's readiness by asking the following questions:

- Do decision participants feel a true stake in the decision?
- Do decision participants share a common purpose and values?
- Do decision participants trust each other, or do they have a desire to create that trust?
- Is every participant willing to put the best interests of the group over his or her personal preferences and self-interests?
- Is it possible to create a meeting environment in which people will share their ideas and opinions freely?
- Are formal leaders prepared to yield to the group's decision on this matter?
- Are people willing to spend the necessary time to let the best decision come about?
- Can the information necessary to make the decision be shared with every member of the group?
- Are decision participants capable of listening well and considering different points of view?
- Do participants possess basic logic and group communication skills, or are they at least open to assistance from a skilled facilitator?

Another important consideration in a group's or organization's readiness for consensus is the willingness of formal and informal leaders to have a "vote" that is no more important than any other stakeholder's vote. When I am speaking with leaders who might be considering using consensus on their team for the first time, I often describe the stakes in this way:

> "Your choice to use consensus means that you will be influencing the conversation based on the merits of your ideas and not based on your position. This means you have to be willing to check your title at the door, along with every other member of the team. Think carefully before you decide to use consensus because there is no faster way to create cynicism than to reverse or veto a consensus decision. You also have a lot to gain by using this method, including a high level of motivation, buy-in, and fast implementation."

As suggested by some of the questions listed previously, an important consideration is the skill level of the group. Consensus involves a variety of critical skills, the most important of which is listening. While anyone can learn consensus building skills, it is important to understand how steep the learning curve is likely to be for any particular group. I have observed that participants often experience consensus as a process of remembering old skills rather than learning new ones. Bad habits die quickly when good ones are rewarded by a satisfying and effective decision-making process.

Decide Who to Involve in the Decision

How do you decide who to involve in a decision? On what basis does a leader make these choices? Here are some useful questions that will help you determine the appropriate group members:

- Who will be most affected by the decision?
- Who will be charged with implementing the decision?
- Whose support is essential to implement the decision?
- What important stakeholders or group perspectives should be represented?

- Who has useful information, experience, or expertise related to this issue?
- Who must be involved to make the decisions resulting from this process credible?

As you identify the people who should be involved in the decision, you will want to consider different kinds of roles. Here are some common ways to distinguish the roles people might play in the decision-making process.

Group Leader. In a hierarchical organization or group, the leader is usually the convener of the decision-making process and the person who has empowered the group to make a consensus-based decision.

Decision Steward. When no one individual is ultimately responsible for the decision, it is useful to have a designated person whose role it is to shepherd the process along. A decision steward may or may not be part of the decision-making group. This person is the official sponsor and coordinator of the process within a community or organization.

Decision Makers. These group members have been authorized to approve the proposal or recommendation that comes out of the group. Without every decision maker's consent, there is no decision.

Advisors. These people bring important information or experience to the group but might not have a strong stake in the decision and do not have a "vote". Advising members can include outside consultants or experts.

Observers. Observers witness the process but do not contribute to the discussion or decision. Typically, observers are expected to remain silent during the meeting(s).

Alternates. For decision processes that may last for several months, it is useful to have alternates who attend all meetings as observers. If the person who the alternate represents is absent, that person takes on decision-maker authority.

Enlist a Skilled Facilitator

The facilitator is an objective, neutral party who is there to help you navigate through the consensus process. An effective facilitator helps your group make decisions that truly reflect the shared will of its members. He or she understands what must occur for consensus to be reached and helps the group increase its ability to make consensus-based decisions. A facilitator should not have a personal stake in the decision or at least should be willing to refrain from expressing personal views to group members.

In consensus, good facilitation can mean the difference between people leaving the meeting energized and committed to the future or feeling tired, frustrated, and defeated.

The consensus facilitator plays an active role before the meeting, helping your group design the overall consensus process. In hierarchical organizations like most companies, an effective facilitator works closely with the group leader to articulate meeting objectives, design agendas, and clarify decision parameters. During the meeting, the facilitator identifies common themes, helps participants synthesize ideas, and creates opportunities for concerns and differences to be expressed.

Some of the functions an experienced facilitator performs include:

- working with the leader and group members to clarify meeting goals and agenda topics
- educating people about how to make consensus decisions
- helping the group establish a shared purpose and ground rules with the group
- fostering a tone of openness that allows for constructive disagreement
- suggesting techniques and tools for decision-making and problem solving

- keeping discussion focused, upbeat, and safe for all participants
- summarizing key discussion points, proposals, and agreements
- encouraging full, balanced participation from all members
- intervening directly or through the group leader to address any disruptive behavior
- helping the group evaluate its effectiveness and learn from its experience

FACILITATOR SELECTION CHECKLIST

- ☐ In-depth knowledge of consensus practices
- ☐ Flexibility in adapting to your group's or organization's unique needs
- ☐ Respect for the time and effort you invest in meetings
- ☐ Ability to listen closely and recognize relationships among ideas
- ☐ Capacity to remain neutral and objective about meeting topics
- ☐ Patience and an outwardly optimistic outlook
- ☐ Focus on what the group needs rather than being liked by its members
- ☐ Experience using approaches that encourage full participation and collaboration
- ☐ Assertiveness and diplomacy in dealing with strong personalities

The division of responsibilities between the facilitator and the leader very much depend on the structure and culture of the organization or decision-making group. Where there is an established structure and an acknowledged leader, the facilitator must be careful not to co-opt the leader's role. I caution facilitators and leaders to keep an eye on "role drift" by ensuring that formal leaders:

- "charter" the decision-making group (see the next section)
- select decision group members
- define meeting objectives and agenda priorities
- open meetings by describing the purpose and objectives
- actively model the ground rules and principles of consensus
- share and ask for observations and feedback about the process
- intervene in concert with the facilitator to end disruptive behavior (see Chapter 5)

Clarify the Group's Scope and Authority

A decision-making group charter defines the group's purpose, authority, values, and operating agreements. Prior to bringing the group together, the group leader or decision steward should take some time to define the charter of the group by answering the following questions:

- What issue is this group being brought together to address?
- Why is this issue important?
- What values must guide any decisions this group makes?
- What are group members' responsibilities?
- How will we know when the group has completed its task?
- Where does this group's decision authority begin and end?
- What are the ground rules for group member behavior?
- How do we define a *consensus decision* in this group?
- What are our time pressures or constraints?
- What happens if we cannot reach agreement by consensus?

DECISION GROUP CHARTER
Spider Corporation's Waste Reduction Task Force

Issue
Our company has set a goal of reducing material we put into the waste stream by 50%. We believe this goal is important because it will enable us to operate more consistently with our company's core value of environmental stewardship. We also believe that reducing waste will reduce operating costs.

Purpose
The purpose of this task force is to develop and recommend to the Executive Committee comprehensive policies and procedures that will result in our waste reduction goal.

Initial Decision Criteria
The task force's recommendation must be guided by the following criteria:
- It is consistent with all of our company's core values.
- It results in the stated goal of 50% waste reduction within 18 months.
- It has a positive or net zero financial impact on company profitability.
- It can be implemented in all of the company's facilities around the country.

Group Authority
This group is charged with developing a consensus-based recommendation (supported by all members of the task force). This recommendation will be brought to the company's Executive Committee for final approval.

Task Force Member Responsibilities
- Attend all meetings, having completed all relevant reading and assignments.
- Advise task force leader if you cannot participate and make arrangements with your alternate.
- Solicit input and feedback from people in your constituency, department, or unit.

Decision Method

The task force will decide on a recommendation by consensus. This means that final recommendation must address every group member's concerns. A consensus decision is more likely to be approved and funded by the Executive Committee. If the group cannot reach consensus, it may submit a description of alternatives considered without a recommendation.

Task Force Parameters

- All dollar expenditures associated with this team's work must be approved by the CFO.
- The Task Force will make recommendations to the Executive Committee by June 15, 2004.

Ground Rules for Member Behavior

To be determined by group at first meeting.

Educate Group Members

In organizations with histories of collaboration and participation, consensus-based decision making is not a big stretch. In organizations where centralized authority (e.g., individual decisions) and competition (e.g., win-lose debate) have been the norm, the learning curve is steeper and more education is required.

With new groups that have very little experience using consensus, I have found that I can lay a solid foundation of principles and practices within ninety minutes. All of the recommended elements for a "consensus briefing" are contained in this book. My strong preference is to co-facilitate this briefing with either the formal leader or the decision steward to demonstrate the organization's commitment to use consensus. Here is a sample agenda for the consensus briefing.

SAMPLE AGENDA FOR CONSENSUS EDUCATION SESSION

A. What is the issue on which we will be deliberating, and why is it significant?* (15 minutes)

B. What is consensus, and why have we chosen to use the method for this decision?* (10 minutes)

C. What are the principles to which we must commit in order to reach true consensus? (15 minutes)

D. What is to be gained if we are successful at reaching consensus?* (5 minutes)

E. What will our process look like? (15 minutes)

F. What are the different roles of people involved in this process? (10 minutes)

G. What are the ground rules? (15 minutes)

H. Where can you learn more about consensus? (5 minutes)

* It is particularly important that this topic be presented by the formal leader or decision steward.

Develop an Agenda

Like most meetings, consensus meetings have a purpose—to make a decision or prepare the group to make a decision. More complex decision processes involve a series of meetings with different purposes. Meeting purposes include:

- Learn about consensus and agree on a work plan.
- Study the issue and arrive at a shared understanding.
- Establish criteria that will be used to develop and select an alternative.
- Generate creative alternatives to address the issue.
- Deliberate and reach a decision.
- Develop a plan for implementing the decision.

For multi-meeting decisions, it is useful to create a road map to which group members can refer during the course of the process. A road map depicts each meeting, clarifies the purpose of the meeting, and shows the relationship among the meetings.

SAMPLE MAP OF MULTI-MEETING DECISION PROCESS:

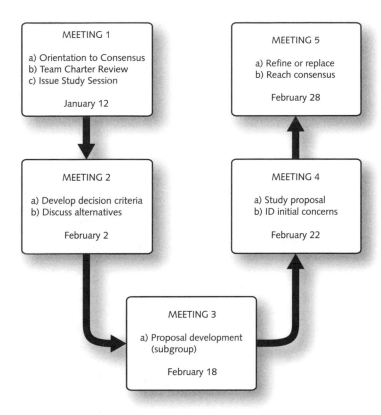

MEETING 1

a) Orientation to Consensus
b) Team Charter Review
c) Issue Study Session

January 12

MEETING 2

a) Develop decision criteria
b) Discuss alternatives

February 2

MEETING 3

a) Proposal development
(subgroup)

February 18

MEETING 4

a) Study proposal
b) ID initial concerns

February 22

MEETING 5

a) Refine or replace
b) Reach consensus

February 28

For any individual meeting, the agenda is a flexible blueprint. It establishes a sequence of topics, defines how much time will be devoted to those topics, and specifies what roles group members will play during different parts of the meeting.

To effectively sequence and allocate time to agenda items, you should consider these six questions:

- Given the purpose and goals of this decision-making group, how relevant is this issue?
- How much time are we likely to need to fully consider and reach a decision on this issue?

- Will we have the information we need to make an informed decision about this item?
- How controversial is this issue likely to be? How much emotion is tied up in this issue?
- Would it be more effective to organize our deliberations on this issue into segments over the course of several meetings?
- What is the importance and urgency of this issue relative to the other items on our agenda?

TIPS FOR AN EFFECTIVE AGENDA

- Avoid lengthy presentations during meetings. Try to distribute information in advance of meetings so that you can use actual meeting time for discussion and decision making.
- Get input from group members who have more experience or knowledge of the issue if you are unsure about the appropriate amount of time for an agenda item.
- Know exactly what "completed" means for every agenda item. Consult with group members to clarify the desired outcome of each agenda item. Participants may describe the following kinds of desired outcomes:
  - We clarified facts and arrived at a shared understanding of . . .
  - We generated ideas for possible solutions to . . .
  - We developed a plan of action for . . .
  - We made a decision about . . .
- Remain flexible. During the meeting, the group may ask you to change the sequence of topics, the amount of time devoted to an item, or the kind of outcome associated with an agenda item.

Gather the Relevant Information

Before the meeting, try to identify relevant information that would be useful in the group's discussion of the issue. Whenever possible, this information should be circulated in advance of the meeting, and group members should be asked to identify clarifying questions and additional information they need.

When the group is at an early phase of understanding an issue, a basic "background briefing" is often useful (see the following template and example). Facts and information can often be provided through expert advisors and fact-finding subgroups comprised of members of the larger consensus group.

ISSUE BRIEFING TEMPLATE

Clarify the issue.
- Describe the situation.
- How long has it been going on?
- What is the history?
- What are the possible causes?

Determine the current impact.
- Who is the issue currently affecting and how?
- How is the issue currently affecting the organization?
- How is the issue currently affecting others (e.g., customers, staff, etc.)?

Determine future implications.
- What is at stake for our organization?
- What is at stake for others outside our organization?
- If nothing changes, what is likely to happen?

Describe the ideal outcome.
- When this issue is resolved, what results do we hope to see?
- How will we know that these results have occurred? How will we measure them?
- In resolving this issue, what principles and goals should guide us?

Identify any preliminary alternatives.
- What are the different approaches that could get us to the resolution described previously?
- What are the pros and cons of each of those alternatives?
- Which alternatives might best achieve the desired outcomes? Why?

This line of questions is based on the "Mineral Rights" model described in *Fierce Conversations* by Susan Scott (New York: Penguin, 2002).

Start the Meeting Off Right

What happens during the first twenty minutes of any meeting lays the foundation for success or failure. By addressing seven key questions at the outset of a consensus meeting, you ensure that participants share a common idea of what is to be accomplished and how it is to be accomplished. In addition to establishing those boundaries, it is also your job as group leader to set a tone that captures the spirit and core values of consensus-based decision-making.

- **Why are we here?** At the outset of the meeting, the group leader (or facilitator if there is no formal leader) provides a concise statement of what the purpose and intended outcomes of the meeting are, including the decisions on which the group will attempt to reach consensus.

  Today you are here to address (name the issue). Specifically, this particular group has been brought together to make a recommendation/decision regarding (name the issue)."

- **What are we authorized to decide?** Clarify the scope of the group's decision-making authority. In most organizations, these parameters are defined by senior management or laid out more formally in the team's charter.

  This group has been charged by (name authorizing person or group) to make a final decision/recommendation regarding (name issue). This group is not authorized to make decisions regarding . . . or decisions that will impact . . ."

- **Who is in the room?** Take some time to make sure all group members, including observers and guests, have a chance to introduce themselves and explain why they are attending.

> Let's take a moment to introduce everyone and to understand why each of you is part of this decision. When you introduce yourself, please state briefly what your connection is to this issue."

- **What special roles will people be playing?** Explain the various roles that people will assume during the decision-making process, including the roles of facilitator, recorder, decision makers, observers, alternates, etc. Explicitly ask group members if they are willing to accept the roles they have been asked to play. This may be a good opportunity to practice a consensus decision!

> As the facilitator, my job is to keep the discussion focused and to make sure everyone has a chance to speak. I'll help weave together the different threads of your discussion to find areas of agreement. In addition, I'll try to highlight points of disagreement and concern. My role is to be neutral regarding the content of your discussion, but to be active in helping you manage the decision process, including enforcing the agreements you'll be making in a little while. Do I have your permission to do this?"

- **Do we understand the consensus process?** Since consensus will be new to many groups, it is important to provide a clear definition of consensus as well as a description of the decision-making process.

> The decisions you are making here today are by consensus. This is a bit different than other decision-making approaches with which you may have been involved. Consensus decisions can only be reached when every one of you states that you've reached a decision you can support—a decision that addresses your concerns and is consistent with the mission, goals, and requirements of the organization. Any questions?"

- **Do we understand the agenda?** Before starting the meeting, describe the agenda. Explain how the time will be allocated for each topic. If any special group processes will be used (e.g., break-out groups), give group members a preview of what this will look like.

> Let me just take a moment to review agenda topics and the time allotted to each topic. Given your purpose and goals for this meeting, does anyone have any reservations or suggestions regarding this agenda?"

- **Are we willing to commit to the ground rules?** Suggest some rules that will guide group member behavior, and ask group members to suggest others they feel would foster a productive and respectful consensus decision process. (See sample ground rules, page 62.)

> I'd like to suggest some agreements that you might adopt. These agreements tend to support effective group decision making and, in particular, consensus. These are 'I' statements because they are commitments each of you makes.
> - I encourage thorough discussion and dissent.
> - I look for common ground solutions by asking 'what if' questions.
> - I do not agree just to avoid conflict.
> - I avoid repeating what has already been said.
>
> Are there other agreements anyone wants to add? (wait for response) Are you willing to keep these agreements in our meeting today? (wait for response) Do I have your permission as facilitator to provide gentle reminders when the agreements are not being kept?" (wait for response)

Careful preparation by enlisting the right people, educating them about consensus decision-making, developing an agenda, and gathering helpful information are among the key steps in helping to ensure an effective process. The next chapter introduces the five basic steps of consensus decision-making.

What Are the Basic Steps?

There are many approaches to consensus decision making, some more complex than others. The following five-step model works well for most decisions.

Step One: Define the Issue

The group first explores the issue or problem it is attempting to address. This phase often involves presentations of related history and background facts. The group's goal during this phase is to develop an informed, shared understanding of the issue and the facts surrounding the issue.

During each step of the consensus process you will find that thoughtful questions can do a lot of the "heavy lifting" for

THE CONSENSUS PROCESS

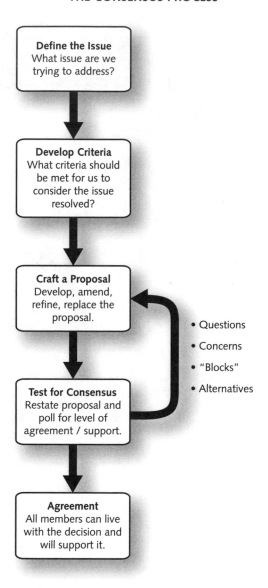

group members. These questions will help the group clearly define the issue:

- Why is this issue important and what exactly is at stake?
- What are the historical, background, and important facts?
- Do we have a common understanding of the facts?
- How is this issue currently affecting our organization?
- What might be the root causes and/or contributing factors?
- What *don't* we know about this issue?
- If nothing changes, what is likely to happen?
- Can we agree on a common statement of the issue or problem?
- Can we state this issue as a "how do we . . . ?" question?

Step Two: Establish Decision Criteria

This is one of the most commonly overlooked steps in consensus decision-making. The more explicit and specific you can be about decision criteria, the easier it is to shape solutions upon which the group can agree.

During this step, the group discusses requirements that any proposal must meet and outcomes that any proposal must achieve. We call these *must* criteria.

Additionally, the group can identify criteria that, while not essential, are desirable. We refer to these criteria as *wants*.

Must criteria are also known as *deal-breaker* criteria because the group will not adopt any proposal that does not meet these criteria. In contrast, *want* criteria are negotiable and cannot be the basis of legitimate opposition.

It is important that decision criteria are articulated clearly and concisely. The following questions will help the group develop its criteria.

- What conditions must be met for this issue to be resolved?
- What do we really want to achieve relative to resolving this issue?
- What shared/organizational interests and needs must be met?

- What resource limitations and/or requirements must be met?
- What shared concerns will a solution need to address?
- What side effects need to be avoided?

WHEN "MUST" CRITERIA ARE IGNORED

A nationwide industry association needed to determine where it would hold its annual trade show. The group developed a set of "must" criteria based on extensive surveying of attendee needs. When it came time to select the city, a coalition of members made an emotional plea for loyalty to a particular city, which had been the historical site of the event. Despite the fact that this city met very few of the group's pre-established "must" criteria, it was chosen to be the site of the trade show. In this case, the decision-making group was convinced by a few members to make its decision based on something other than the criteria established through extensive research and deliberation. The decision was disconnected from what had been defined as "the best interests of the organization and its stakeholders."

One board member described the impact of ignoring the decision criteria in this way:

"We made this decision based on emotion rather than on what made sense. Now we are paying the price. Our ability to achieve the organization's goals continues to be limited by our choice of locations."

Step Three: Craft the Proposal

As indicated by the flow chart at the beginning of this chapter, consensus is an iterative process of crafting an initial proposal and then refining or sometimes replacing that proposal to address legitimate concerns of group members.

Drafting a Preliminary Proposal

An initial written proposal is usually drafted after criteria are defined and agreed upon. This can be done by the entire group or by a designated member or subgroup. Putting together a preliminary proposal may take some time and creativity. It often involves consulting with people with a stake in the decision about alternative solutions, testing ideas, hearing concerns, and conducting research.

The time invested in this step is well spent. A well-articulated preliminary proposal focuses the group's discussion without necessarily advocating endorsement of the proposal.

Building Group Ownership

Avoid attributing authorship of the initial proposal. This enables the *group* to assume ownership of the ideas in the proposal as "our work in progress." As changes are suggested and subsequent proposals are developed, continue to avoid crediting authorship to individuals or subgroups.

Pose the following questions to assist the group in crafting its initial proposals.

- What ideas do people have about solutions that would meet our criteria?
- What do these alternative ideas share in common?
- Can any of these ideas be combined?
- Can we make this solution simpler, less expensive, and/or faster to implement?
- What options haven't we explored?

Asking Clarifying Questions

Once the proposal has been developed, it is presented to the group. During the presentation, limit discussion to *clarifying questions*. The following clarifying questions seek to confirm understanding of the proposal and make any assumptions explicit:

- What would help you better understand this proposal?
- What isn't clear to you?
- What would enable you to explain this proposal to someone outside of this group?

- What are the stated and unstated assumptions of this proposal?
- Do we have a shared common understanding of the proposal?

Step Four: Test for Consensus

This is the most critical step of the consensus process and the one that requires the most skill. Once a proposal has been presented to the group and all clarifying questions have been answered, it is time to test for consensus. Testing for consensus involves asking every member of the group to state his or her level of comfort with and support for the proposal, based on the shared goals and criteria the group established during Step 2 (Chapter 4 is dedicated to this step in the process). During Step 4, it is important to be clear that you are asking group members to weigh in on the specific proposal.

You are **NOT** asking
- *Is this your first choice?*
- *Does this meet your personal needs and interests?*

You **ARE** asking
- *Is this a proposal with which you can live and ultimately support?*
- *Does it meet the shared criteria for the group?*
- *Do you believe this proposal represents the group's best thinking at this time?*
- *Is this the best decision for our organization and its stakeholders?*

In asking people to weigh in on their level of comfort and support for a proposal, there are several possible outcomes.

Scenario 1. Every member of the group feels comfortable and supportive of the proposal. No one raises concerns or opposition. Consensus is reached relatively quickly.

Scenario 2. Some members of the group support the proposal. Other members have concerns or questions. Over the course of discussion, the group refines the proposal and provides information in ways that allow concerned members to support the proposal. Consensus is reached.

Scenario 3. In addition to concerns, some members oppose the proposal based on their sense either that it cannot fulfill one of the agreed-upon must criteria or that it somehow violates the organization's purpose or goals. This type of legitimate opposition, also known as a *block,* can trigger creative discussion in which the group searches for new solutions. If a new solution is found that addresses all member concerns, consensus is reached. (See Chapter 4 for more on dealing with legitimate blocks.)

Scenario 4. Sometimes a group is unable to find a way to address concerns and/or opposition. If the group cannot formulate a proposal that every member can support, consensus agreement is not reached.

Step Five: Reach Agreement

Consensus is achieved when every member of the group indicates that they believe the proposal represents the best thinking of the group at this time and that it addresses all legitimate concerns raised.

In doing a final check for consensus, it is useful to restate the proposed decision and ask each member of the group:

Are you comfortable that this decision is the best decision for the organization and its stakeholders at this time, and are you prepared to support its implementation?

Formalizing the Consensus Agreement

Once a consensus decision is made and a written record of the decision completed, I like to have group members sign the final proposal or decision report. The signature is a formal way for members to indicate their intentions to actively support implementation.

SAMPLE DECISION STATEMENT

On March 31, 2006, the Yummy Muffin Marketing Task Force (comprised of executives from corporate marketing and our largest franchise owners) reached consensus on the selection of an advertising agency that will handle our national marketing campaign. After an exhaustive search and a competition among four national agencies, we selected Boll Creative based on the following criteria:

- Creative capability as demonstrated in the television and print competition
- Capacity to create an integrated campaign using television, radio, print, and direct mail
- Understanding of our industry and its consumers
- Experience in negotiating competitive media buys
- Competitive pricing of the proposal relative to others considered
- Stability and track record of the agency

As a result of this decision, the members of the Marketing Task Force are fully committed to moving forward with Boll Creative.

When Groups Cannot Reach Consensus

There will be times when a group cannot find a way to address concerns or resolve a legitimate block in the time it has to make a decision. This is a completely reasonable way for a consensus process to end. However, when consensus cannot be reached, alternatives do exist. These alternatives are also known as *fallbacks*. Although it is useful to have a fallback position identified in advance, it is my experience that given enough time and the right intention, consensus can be reached most of the time. That said, here is a brief description of some alternatives to use when consensus is not possible.

Defer the Decision. If there is not an urgent need to reach a decision, a group may decide simply to defer the decision until circumstances change or new information is brought to light.

Since the homeowners' association could not reach consensus on whether to build a swimming pool, the membership decided to defer the decision and take it up again next year.

Give Decision Authority to a Subgroup. The group may determine in advance that if the larger group is unable to reach consensus, the final decision will be delegated to a smaller subgroup.

The members of the homeowners' association designated a five-member group to make a final decision about the pool based on the criteria and guidelines provided by the larger membership.

Push the Decision Upward. In hierarchical organizations, a decision may be pushed up to an individual manager or executive group. A full summary of the alternatives considered, proposals, concerns, and reason for any opposition are provided to the decision makers who may or may not have been involved in the group's deliberations.

The homeowners' association empowered its three-member Executive Board to make a final decision between two attractive options that had been developed.

Seek Mediation. If some members are holding out for legitimate reasons, it is sometimes useful to employ a trained mediator to work specifically with those group members who hold differences. Mediation is a structured process through which individuals are encouraged to air their views and work toward resolution of differences. A mediator is particularly useful when emotions are running high and individuals are not feeling that their perspective is being heard. Like group facilitators, mediators never take a position on the topic under dispute. According to the Mediation Network of North Carolina, the mediator works to:

- Facilitate communication among the parties
- Help them explore mutual understanding
- Assist them in defining and clarifying issues
- Maximize the exploration of alternatives
- Assist in exploring reconciliation and settlement

Example: The homeowners whose house would be adjacent to the swimming pool were vehemently opposed to the idea. All other members were in favor. The group called in a mediator to ensure that the opposing members' perspective was fully heard and to explore whether those concerns could somehow be addressed.

At its most basic, the consensus process entails defining the issue, developing decision criteria, crafting a proposal, testing for consensus, and reaching agreement or an alternative conclusion. The next chapter addresses a common occurrence in consensus decision-making—a cycle of disagreement and discovery that can produce frustration or innovative solutions.

How Do I Work with Disagreement?

The most exciting and creative part of the consensus process is when a group is cycling between Steps 3 and 4. Proposals are made, concerns are raised, and the group attempts to refine or replace the proposal to address those concerns. During this part of the consensus process, groups can experience fruitful innovation or intense frustration. Often, they experience both. I call this *the cycle of disagreement and discovery.*

Using Consensus Cards

I created a tool called *Consensus Cards*™* to maximize focus, creativity, and respect. The method is simple to use. Provide each

*See Resource Guide.

THE CONSENSUS PROCESS WITH CYCLE OF DISAGREEMENT

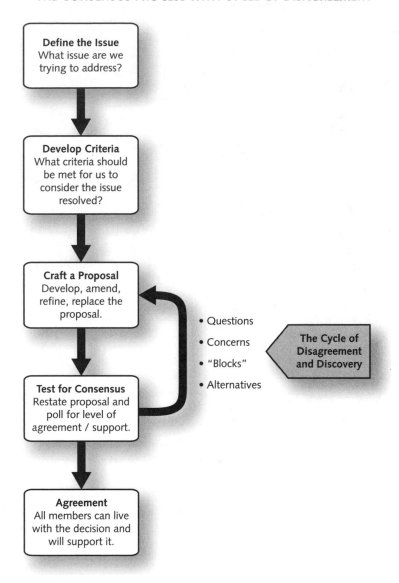

group member with three cards: one green card, one yellow card, and one red card. The cards are large enough to be seen across the room or conference table.

After a proposal is presented to the group and all clarifying questions have been addressed, the facilitator asks participants to indicate their level of comfort and support for the proposal by holding up one of the three cards.

Each card color signifies a different level of support for the proposal:

Green. I support this proposal. This is the best decision we can arrive at for our organization and its stakeholders at this time.

Yellow. I could support this proposal. I have some questions and/or concerns I need to have addressed.

Red. I do not support this proposal. It does not serve the best interests of our organization and its stakeholders at this time.

Once all group members have held up their cards, each card holder has a specific role:

Green Card Holders

Once every group member is showing a card, advise green card holders that their job is to remain quiet and listen carefully to the concerns and ideas of members holding yellow and red cards.

> ▶ Supporters of the proposal (green card holders) are asked to remain silent to eliminate what is often a time-consuming series of endorsement speeches and sales pitches.

Yellow Card Holders

Ask each yellow card holder to describe his or her concern and record concerns on a flip chart. The facilitator's job is to consolidate all concerns and get a sense from the card holder whether the concern is a *must* or a *want.* If the *want* is not resolved by the group, the card holder may still be willing to "go green" as long as the concern is put on the meeting record.

Once all concerns have been identified and recorded, any group member can respond with information or suggested refinements to the proposal that might address the concern. As each member's concerns are resolved, they are asked to show a green card.

Red Card Holders
After all major concerns are expressed and resolved, the facilitator asks holders of red cards to state the source of their opposition and describe their proposed alternative. If the alternative proposal appears to meet the group's decision criteria, the facilitator may poll group members on this proposal using the Consensus Cards.

> Red card holders should be strongly encouraged to offer one or more alternative proposals that address their reasons for opposition.

In the following sections, we will explore how to work constructively with people who are expressing legitimate concerns (yellow card holders) and opposition (red card holders).

Expressing and Resolving Legitimate Concerns
In consensus, each group member has the right and responsibility to express concerns he or she has about any proposal. Legitimate concerns often take the form of questions and statements about aspects of the proposal that might not serve the organization's best interests. As concerns are raised, it is the group's job to understand and attempt to resolve them.

As a facilitator, you need to allow as much time as necessary for every member of the group to state his or her concerns. It is also important for the facilitator to create a safe environment in which no concern is minimized or dismissed.

As each concern is identified, list them on a flip chart. Because consensus requires that every legitimate concern be addressed, there is no need to vote on or agree with concerns as they are identified. Simply record every concern as it is raised and make sure that the concern falls into the definition of "legitimate."

> One way to test whether a concern is legitimate is to ask: "Is this concern based on our group's purpose, a shared value, or one of our decision criteria, or is it an individual member's need or preference?"

Legitimate concerns from group members can be resolved in three ways:

- Provide additional information so that the person raising the concern feels it has been addressed. (Example: Tom's concern about the new employee benefits policy was based on a false assumption that hourly workers would not qualify. Once Jane clarified that hourly employees would be eligible, Tom withdrew his concern.)
- Refine the proposal in either a small or significant way to address the concern. (Example: Fran raised a concern that the new benefits policy would take effect mid-year and could create an inconvenience for employees with regard to their taxes. As a result of this concern, the launch date was set for January 1 of next year.)
- Offer this option to the person raising the concern: He or she can ask to have the concern made part of the meeting record but agree to fully support the decision. In doing so, the group member is saying, "I have a concern, but even if we are not able to resolve it, I believe that our current proposal represents the group's best thinking at this time so I will support the decision."

The process of addressing concerns has been described as a creative search for *a third way,* which lies somewhere between right/wrong, either/or, and good/bad answers.

The consensus dialogue almost always leads to a more clearly articulated, higher-quality solution with stronger commitment behind it. The following questions will help the group resolve concerns and reach agreement on a proposal.

- Is there anyone who cannot live with this version of the proposal?
- Can anyone offer further improvements to the proposal?
- Have all concerns been addressed?
- Does this concern fall within our purpose, values, and decision criteria?
- Must this concern be resolved for you to support the proposal, or would you simply *prefer* to have it resolved?
- Can we refine the proposal to remove the issues that are holding us up?
- Can anyone offer further improvements?
- Can anyone suggest a way to proceed that meets all concerns we have heard expressed?
- What improvements or changes can you suggest to the current proposal that will make it more acceptable to you while continuing to meet the *must* criteria we have set?
- Is there information or advice we could get from outside the group that might help resolve this concern?

Dealing with Opposition or "Blocks"

What makes consensus unique and profoundly democratic is that each group member has the option and responsibility to block a proposal if he or she believes it does not serve the best interests of the group. Blocking is a way for any member to stop a proposal from moving forward.

Legitimate Opposition
A member may legitimately block a decision if he or she believes that the proposed solution will be bad for the organization and

sees no way of modifying it to prevent the negative impact. Some legitimate reasons to block or "red card" a decision include:

- The proposal fails to meet one or more of the *must* criteria developed by the group.
- The proposal is not consistent with the organization's mission and/or values.
- The proposal violates the law or some shared and widely accepted standard of ethics.

A legitimate block, when dealt with effectively, can lead to more creative, effective decisions. Group members should embrace rather than resent legitimate opposition. Raising a legitimate block can take a great deal of courage and commitment. Remember the film *Twelve Angry Men*? The character played by Henry Fonda blocked an entire jury's decision because he believed the jury members were rushing toward an unjust verdict based on criteria that were not consistent with the legal standard for justice and "must" criteria, guilty beyond a reasonable doubt.

Some of the most innovative and effective decisions I have facilitated have come about in response to a consensus block.

▶ The facilitator's job is to help the group see a legitimate block as an opportunity to look for an entirely new and creative solution.

When the group is faced with the task of searching for alternatives to the proposed decision, these questions are useful.

- What elements of previous proposals would be acceptable to all of us?
- Other than this proposal, which alternative is most attractive?
- What would be an entirely new way to approach this issue?

Nonlegitimate or Obstructive Opposition

In consensus, an individual cannot block a decision simply because he or she does not like it. One of the most common errors is a block based on a group member's personal values, beliefs, or interests. This kind of block is not legitimate in the context of a consensus-based decision process. When a nonlegitimate block occurs, the group should immediately attempt to distinguish between shared and individual decision criteria, goals, and interests.

If you hear any of these reasons for a block, it is likely not to be legitimate in the context of consensus.

- *This proposal does not fit with my personal values, beliefs, or needs.*
- *This proposal is not my first choice or preference.*
- *I have a personal interest that is not being taken into account.*
- *I don't like the way Joe is treating me in this meeting and I'm not going to agree to anything until I get respect.*
- *I can't explain why I'm against it. I just am.*

Blocking should be virtually unnecessary if your group has done its homework prior to the meeting. Have you established clearly stated, shared decision criteria? Gathered good information on which to base the proposal? Solicited input from people during the development of the proposal?

Individual members are less likely to block if they have had adequate time to understand the proposal, express concerns, and work through those concerns. Nonlegitimate blocks are less likely when the group environment is based on shared purpose, trust, and openness.

OPPOSITION BASED ON PERSONAL VALUES

A few years ago, I served on a not-for-profit organization's Board of Directors. The board was discussing an opportunity for a large grant. The source of the grant was a local company that happened to be a subsidiary of a multinational cigarette manufacturer. Our organization had never declined a donation and had no criteria for doing so. In the meeting, I opposed the contribution based on my personal disapproval of the tobacco industry as well as the company's unethical policies over the years. Other members of the board considered my views quite carefully.

The facilitator asked board members to consider whether we wanted to set a policy regarding the kinds of money we would not accept. This led to a very important discussion. In the end, board members decided they did not feel such a guideline was in the best interest of the organization at this time, and there was no shared value regarding the tobacco industry or any other industry. At that point, I had to acknowledge that my opposition was grounded in personal values, not organizational values. I also decided that I could continue to serve on the board even if we were not aligned on this particular value.

The accompanying case on my experience with a nonprofit board illustrates what Quakers would call "standing aside." Standing aside is an important alternative for decision stakeholders because it gives one a way to go on record with a strong personal concern while enabling them to avoid taking an obstructionist position. People who stand aside are usually saying: "I have a strong objection to the proposal based on my personal beliefs or values. I do not have enough supportive energy to assist with implementation, nor will I obstruct it in any way." If more than one person or an individual whose support is essential for implementation stands aside on a decision, it is advisable for the facilitator to keep the group in deliberation mode.

Although individual values may not be a legitimate basis on which to block a decision, they are always worth raising. As illustrated in this case example, raising a concern based on an individual member's values may provoke an important discussion that clarifies the group's goals and convictions.

The central theme of this chapter is that, when effectively handled, disagreement can produce discovery. Group members should be encouraged to raise legitimate concerns, so the group can understand and attempt to resolve them. Group members have a responsibility to block a decision for legitimate reasons, but not simply because they do not like it.

CHAPTER 5

Six Traps That Undermine Consensus

Group facilitation is an art, and facilitating consensus-based decisions is the pinnacle of that art form. It can be one of the most challenging types of decision processes to facilitate—and one of the most rewarding.

The more you facilitate consensus-based processes, the more likely you are to encounter "traps" that have the potential to cause an unnecessary breakdown in the process. Not every consensus process leads to a consensus decision. As described in Chapter 4, there are legitimate reasons consensus is not reached. That said, you must learn to recognize and constructively address disruptive behaviors that undermine the spirit and practice of consensus.

Let's examine some of the most common traps that have the potential to undermine a consensus process.

Member Absence from Critical Meetings

Occasionally, a group member shows up to a meeting after missing one or more important discussions. This member expects to participate in the decision despite the fact that he or she has not been privy to important facts and perspectives shared at previous meetings. Valuable time can be wasted attempting to bring this person up to speed. Worse still, the individual may take an inflexible stand based on an uninformed premise.

Ways to Prevent and/or Intervene

- When you charter the group, establish an agreement up front about attendance. Identify a standard of meeting attendance that qualifies a member to participate in decisions. Members who exceed the standard may still participate in discussion and express opinions but must abstain from actual decision approval.
- Put a procedure in place whereby absent members must proactively seek to be briefed in writing, in person by another member, or both prior to the following meeting. Members who do not avail themselves of the briefing lose their role in decision-making.
- Designate "alternate" representatives. An alternate is particularly useful when the decision process is likely to last for several months. Alternates attend all meetings as observers when the primary representative is present. If that member is absent, the alternate becomes a decision maker.

Grandstanding Members

You may have participated in meetings during which a dominant or outspoken member repeatedly raised the same issue over and over again, even after it had been addressed. This kind of person sometimes becomes argumentative, repeats the same point over and over again, or takes illogical stances. The grandstanding member is often looking for attention or using the group to work out a personal issue unrelated to the group's purpose.

Ways to Prevent and/or Intervene

- Determine whether the concern repeatedly raised by the dominant member is relevant to the group's purpose and decision criteria. If it is, ask group members to provide facts and information that will address it. If it is not relevant, explain why.

- As a facilitator, record the person's point and acknowledge that it has been heard and how it was addressed. If necessary, interrupt and ask group members whether they feel the issue has been addressed. Gently remind the person of the ground rule regarding repeating oneself.

> "Thanks, Sally. I've heard you mention the safe drinking water issue three times and I want to point out that we have recorded the issue as you described it up here on the flip chart. Just as we've heard what matters to you, I want to make sure that we hear from everyone today. We've invested the last 15 minutes exploring with you how this issue is connected to the decision this group is charged with making today. Here's what we heard . . . Are you satisfied that we have heard you? I'm sensing that the group is ready to move beyond this issue. Is that correct? OK, then let's hear from the people who have been less vocal so far."

- If the dominant member persists, indicate that each member has taken responsibility for abiding by the agenda and ground rules. Suggest that it is important to move forward. Ask the individual to withdraw from the group unless he or she is willing to participate cooperatively.

Obstructive Blocking

In the previous chapter we defined *legitimate blocking* as opposition based on criteria and goals that are shared by the group. This form of opposition is an appropriate and common part of consensus. While it is the right of every group member to challenge any proposal, it is also the responsibility of the group as a whole to determine whether the opposition is legitimate.

Obstructive blocks are most commonly based on personal interests or needs. Obstructive blockers may refuse to allow ideas other than their own to be considered. This kind of opposition violates the spirit of consensus and has the potential to hijack the process.

Ways to Prevent and/or Intervene

- Be sure to give the concern a fair hearing. Test the facts and assumptions behind the concern (see questions on page 48). Remind participants that consensus means committing to a decision that is in the *shared interests of the group*. Ask how the reasons for opposition are connected to the group's decision criteria and shared interests.

- Explore whether the block has to do with individual preferences or values that may differ from the organization's or group's values. Sometimes a significant gap between a group member and organizational values results in the departure of the member or a reexamination of the group's shared values. (See Case Example on page 50.)

- Occasionally, a group member is unwilling to see that the source of his or her opposition is not appropriate for a consensus process (See definition of *legitimate block* on page 49), no matter how clearly the principles and ground rules were described. In these cases, a difficult decision must be made to ask the member to leave the group. This should be done in a way that preserves the individual's dignity and reduces the possibility of public embarrassment.

Pablo, the group respects your personal convictions about veg-
etarianism and would neither impose nor require you to live in
a way that does not have integrity for you. And at this time,
this grocery store has not made the philosophical choice to
exclude meat products from our merchandise selection. The
store's mission is to offer 'healthy, organic foods,' which
includes organic, range-fed meats. Today we are trying to
select product within the scope of our existing values and
criteria. Though we have asked today, I have not heard any
members of the Product Advisory Committee express support
for the position that we should reexamine our mission and
product selection criteria. It is the kind of philosophical question
you would need to raise with the Board of Directors. Until our
mission and product criteria change, we can't accept your reasons for blocking this particular decision."

Pressuring Members to Conform
(Coercive Tactics)

Sometimes members make it difficult for other members to
express legitimate concerns or opposition. Dissenting members
are made to feel that they are "getting in the way of agreement"
or "bogging down the decision-making process." Sometimes
coercive members apply explicit or subtle pressure on dissenting
members to conform to the majority's wishes. The danger of
coercive tactics is that they can result in tacit agreement without
true support for a decision.

WHEN PERSONAL INTERESTS INTERFERE

Members of a vendor selection team were debating which supplier
would be awarded a multimillion-dollar service contract. Several members of the team appeared to be favoring a vendor that met very few of

the team's established criteria. They took strong and seemingly irrational positions in favor of this vendor. They engaged in bullying tactics both during and outside of the team's meetings. It was finally discovered that these members had accepted large "gifts" from the vendor they favored. They were disqualified from participating in the decision.

Ways to Prevent and/or Intervene

- At the outset of the process, emphasize that each member has not only the right, but also the *responsibility* to express concerns or opposition to a proposal. Remind group members that they are involved in a collaborative search for a solution that meets the group's interests. Most importantly, advise the team that constructive challenges raise the level of decision quality and creativity.

- If you observe group members being pressured to conform, point it out and redirect members' attention to addressing the legitimate concerns being raised. Remind the group that decisions based on pressure to conform are not sustainable because they have no commitment behind them.

Group Fatigue and/or Frustration

As a general rule, the more complex and controversial a decision, the longer it takes to reach consensus. During the course of a meeting, members may become fatigued. As participants become tired, they often become frustrated, impatient, and argumentative—not exactly the ingredients of which great decisions are made.

Ways to Prevent and/or Intervene

- In planning the agenda, anticipate decisions that may require a multi-step approach. If necessary, get support for a series of meetings rather than just a single event.

- Express encouragement and optimism. Acknowledge and legitimize the frustration (*I know this is difficult work and see that you are frustrated at this moment*). Remind partici-

pants of the importance of their goal and encourage them to
stay with it.

- Mirror the comments back to the group and ask for suggestions. (*You've said that you are frustrated with the slow
  pace. Any suggestions of ways we might move forward more
  efficiently?*) Offer your own observations and ideas based on
  what you hear.

- Remind the group why it has chosen a consensus approach
  and how it is likely to pay off in the long run. (*The time you
  invest trying to figure out a decision you can all support will
  pay off when it comes time to implement.*) Show them the
  progress they have made so far and how each agreement
  builds on the next.

- If you feel the meeting is bogging down because members do
  not have adequate process skills, evaluate the meeting with
  the group to identify what they might need to learn. Consider inserting some training on good consensus or meeting
  practices.

Silent Members

Group members, particularly members of a minority constituency, do not always feel comfortable expressing concerns,
offering ideas, or challenging proposals that appear to have
majority group support. Additionally, some people simply do not
feel comfortable speaking in large groups. If members do not
express themselves during the decision-making process, they are
likely to leave the meeting less than committed to decisions.

Ways to Prevent and/or Intervene

- Conduct a premeeting survey to identify general concerns
  and suggestions about the proposal. Summarize these for the
  group without attributing the comments.

- Provide opportunities for smaller group discussion. After
  small groups have discussed a question, they assign a

spokesperson to present their ideas and perspectives to the larger group.

- If you notice that certain group members are particularly quiet, check in with them during a break to determine whether there is something they want to say but are unable or unwilling to do so. Remind them of their responsibility to voice their opinions and encourage them to either raise the issue themselves or find someone to raise it on their behalf.

- Use a "round robin" approach. For important questions or decision points, you may ask each member to express an opinion by simply going around the table or room. Even in this process, participants should be given the option to "pass" if they truly have nothing to say on the topic.

Whether dealing with a grandstander, shy group member, or someone who is chronically absent, it is often useful and appropriate for you to explore with the member how his or her behavior serves the best interests of the group.

As we have seen in this chapter, several traps can undermine consensus, from members who miss critical meetings, grandstand, or raise nonlegitimate blocks to group fatigue and frustration. A facilitator can help groups steer clear of these traps by reminding members of the ground rules and keeping the focus on the basic, constructive steps of consensus. The next chapter offers recommendations for effective consensus meetings.

CHAPTER

Ten Tips for Better Consensus Meetings

Every group facilitator has a favorite set of tools and techniques for helping people collaborate effectively. Here are ten tips I believe are most useful in consensus-based decision processes.

When and how you use these suggestions should be informed by your own style and intuition. For example, I can't tell you exactly when to use silence or a meeting break as an intervention. This is a judgment you will gain through your own experience and experimentation. Additionally, these tips are not intended to be formulas or templates. In fact, I encourage you to modify them so that they become authentic expressions of your own unique approach to facilitation.

Set Clear Ground Rules

Ground rules are shared agreements about acceptable group member behavior. In fact, this is often the first consensus-based decision a group is asked to make. Ground rules create a collective standard for behavior and therefore enable the facilitator or other group members to intervene when they are not being followed. Each group should create its own ground rules so that group members feel a sense of ownership and commitment to them.

SAMPLE CONSENSUS GROUND RULES

- ☐ Share ideas openly and succinctly.
- ☐ Listen openly to ideas, concerns, and criticism from others.
- ☐ Express disagreement and concerns constructively.
- ☐ Avoid arguing for my own position or idea.
- ☐ Decide based on what is best for the organization.
- ☐ Look for common ground solutions by asking "what if" questions.
- ☐ Consent only when a proposal makes sense to me.
- ☐ Withdraw concerns as they are addressed.
- ☐ Ask questions to uncover important information and assumptions.
- ☐ Actively encourage others to speak.
- ☐ Accept criticism and disagreement as a constructive source of input.
- ☐ Pause to reflect on what has been said before sharing ideas.
- ☐ Avoid repeating what has already been said.
- ☐ Do not agree just to avoid conflict.
- ☐ Encourage thorough discussion and dissent.

Use a "Group Memory"

Designate a scribe or recorder to take notes on a flip chart. Whenever possible, ask a neutral party (e.g., someone who is not involved in the decision) to play this role. The recorder takes notes on a flip chart or some other medium that is visible to all group members. As the discussion evolves, members can refer to the record to confirm what has been said and agreed upon.

A group memory is particularly useful when developing decision criteria, listing concerns, categorizing ideas, and refining proposals. Make sure that the person taking notes limits the amount of paraphrasing and checks in with group members to confirm accuracy.

Before any final consensus decision, a written version of the proposal should be presented so that group members can review the specific language. After meetings, the recorder transcribes the notes and distributes them as meeting minutes.

Distinguish "Must" from "Want" Criteria

As the group identifies the criteria upon which it will evaluate any proposals (see page 35 for a description of this step in the process), it is important that a distinction be made between *must* and *want* criteria. As a reminder, *must* criteria, also known as "deal-breakers," are standards that the proposal must meet to be adopted by the group. *Want* criteria may be desirable but are not essential to a consensus decision. Additionally, some *want* criteria are more important than others. In some cases, it is useful to designate high, medium, and low importance to each *want* criteria.

Use Silence and Pauses

There are very useful ways to employ silence as a tool in consensus building. First, build in a group norm of pausing for 15 to 30 seconds after each person speaks. A short yet significant pause provides participants the opportunity to reflect on what has been said and decide what they think about an idea that has been shared. This practice decreases the prevalence of shoot-from-the-hip responses and interruptions. It creates a more respectful environment in which ideas are fully considered.

A second way to use silence is to suggest a prolonged period (5 to 15 minutes) of quiet reflection after a presentation or discussion. This is a particularly effective intervention when the discussion seems to have hit a dead-end or members are becoming otherwise frustrated. Extended silence is different from a break because you are specifically asking people to "work individually" on the problem at hand. Before suggesting a prolonged pause, it is useful to summarize where the discussion is at and provide clear questions on which participants can reflect.

> Here's a summary of the current proposal. The concerns identified are . . . and the suggestions provided thus far for addressing those concerns are . . . I'd like to suggest that we take 10 minutes to individually reflect on this question (written on a flip chart): What modified or entirely new proposal will address the remaining concerns? If it's helpful, please feel free to take notes as you think about this question on your own.

Assign Questions and Tasks to Breakout Groups

With groups of more than ten people, it is useful at times to split the group into triads or small groups. Define a question or task, and ask each group to work on theirs and present their work to the larger group.

Breakout groups often produce a greater diversity of ideas since there is less opportunity for "group think" to develop. Another advantage of breakout groups is that they enable people who do not feel comfortable speaking in the larger group to participate.

Put the Discussion in a Fishbowl

In larger groups it is often difficult to hear opinions from every member on every issue. Fishbowl discussions enable different viewpoints to be discussed and debated while others listen and reflect on what is being said. The facilitator selects four or five group members who represent different perspectives on a question (e.g., *What should our decision criteria include?*). These members are then asked to discuss the question from their perspective as the rest of the group observes the discussion.

In some versions of fishbowls, members from the outer (observer) circle can tap inside circle members on the shoulder as a signal that they would like to rotate into the fishbowl and express a perspective that has not yet been stated.

At the conclusion of the fishbowl discussion, all members of the group discuss what they have heard and identify the most important insights and ideas. This technique is particularly useful for simultaneously exploring an issue in depth while enabling other group members to critically consider what is said.

Stack Participants

When several members want to speak at the same time, this is a useful method for bringing order to the conversation. Stacking simply involves assigning an order to who will speak next.

> OK, I can see that several people want to speak on this topic. Let's go around the table and create a sequence. John, why don't you speak first? Then let's hear from Frank, Samantha, and Linda, in that order. Does anyone else want to be included in this round of comments? Just let me know and we will put you into the mix."

As the facilitator, remain neutral with regard to whom you select to speak and where you place them in the sequence of speakers. Call on people by alternating between ends of the conference table or corners of the room so that your neutrality is transparent to others.

Stacking reassures participants that they will have an opportunity to speak and enables them to focus on what others are saying rather than spending their energy looking for an opening to speak. However, stacking can also be too structured when a conversation calls for more fluid give and take on a particular topic.

Take a Break

There have been dozens of times when I have worked with a group that had reached a critical impasse. The group was struggling to refine its proposal in a way that resolved important concerns or overcame strong sources of opposition. In such moments, people are usually feeling fatigued, patience is running short, and some folks may be feeling resentful of those people who cannot support the proposal. In these moments, I have found that the best thing I can do for the group is to call for a 10- or 15-minute break. In addition to providing people with an opportunity to stretch their legs, use the restroom, and get refreshments, this *timeout* serves to relieve some of the accumulated tension in the room.

Breaks also give people a chance to connect with one another on a personal level. These more intimate conversations often mitigate interpersonal differences and build bridges that enable a group to get to consensus more quickly.

Use Technology Wisely

Tools like e-mail, online surveys, real-time text messaging, and blogs have become a way of life in an age of high technology. With geographically dispersed teams and global organizations on the rise, technology makes it possible for us to share ideas and make decisions together even though we are not in the same room. These tools enable us to deliberate and decide across time zones, physical distances, and even languages.

While exchanging ideas via text can create a sense of neatness, precision, and objectivity, some important elements can get lost in the transmission—emotion, relationship, shared understanding, ownership, and a willingness to be influenced by others. These key ingredients for high commitment decisions are especially vulnerable when using text-based technology and need to be safeguarded. When considering the use of technology in a consensus decision process, consider the following questions:

At this stage of the process, will the use of a particular technology enhance or inhibit

- people's opportunity to be heard and equally influence the process?
- the expression of important nuances and emotions associated with the issue?
- the use of disagreement as a positive force and a source for creative thinking?
- a decision that serves the interests and needs of the whole group?

My recommendation: When a group needs to make a high-stakes decision, try to make it via simultaneous face-to-face, eye-to-eye, voice-to-voice communication. When gathering all of the decision makers in the same room is not possible, I favor phone or video conferencing. Here are some dos and don'ts for the use of technology when real-time personal communication is not possible.

DO	DON'T
• Use e-mail, online surveys, and blogs to gather people's ideas and perspectives in advance of more personal interaction (e.g., a meeting, phone conference, or video conference). • Have the group commit to a set of "best practices" for text communication. These include using precise language, asking about others' perspectives, balancing criticism with appreciation, avoiding grandstanding or repeating the same point, and qualifying the tone of one's comments when there is a possibility it might be misinterpreted. • When all decision participants have access to computers and deliberating from a distance is the only option, consider using web-enabled meeting tools that provide you with the ability to talk on the phone while reviewing and refining a shared work product online.	• Use computer-based technology when some of the decision participants lack ready access to or experience with a computer. • Attempt to hold a prolonged deliberation or make a complex decision via e-mail, text messaging, or blog. • Use polling and decision-making software programs that encourage people to be in the same room, while engaged with a computer screen rather than with each other and expressing anonymous opinions rather than owning their ideas. • Reply immediately if you are tempted to respond emotionally or are making assumptions about others' motives. • Confront people who are not following the rules described in the "dos" column via e-mail (a personal phone call or face-to-face discussion is best in this situation).

Evaluate the Meeting

The way that groups improve their ability to make consensus decisions is with practice and reflection. Plan a 10-minute segment at the conclusion of the meeting to discuss how the process went. This is an opportunity for group members to comment on what they are observing and learning. Participants will typically raise issues and questions related to meeting process, behavior of group members, tone of the meeting, and level of satisfaction with the outcomes.

The meeting evaluation is not a time to revisit any of the substantive decisions or topics covered during the meeting. An effective evaluation will help participants identify what went right and think about how to improve those things that did not go well for the next meeting. At the conclusion of the evaluation discussion, the facilitator should summarize what has been said and help the group translate those insights into commitments for future meetings.

SAMPLE DECISION PROCESS EVALUATION

☐ What were the most satisfying outcomes of this meeting?

☐ What was least satisfying?

☐ Thinking about the way we approached shared decision making, what did we do well?

☐ What could we improve upon and how?

☐ What commitments can we make for improving the way we make decisions together?

The tips offered in this chapter are useful steps you can take to ensure that group meetings do not get bogged down or side-tracked. Taking time to complete an evaluation at your final meeting gives members an opportunity to identify where improvements could be made. The following chapter returns to the roots of consensus and shares a more personal perspective on the effective use of this decision-making process.

CHAPTER 7

Toward High-Commitment Decisions

Making the choice to bring people together—to decide together—is an act of courage for a leader. It is a bold and, in some corners, radical admission that formal leaders don't have all the answers. It is recognition that sometimes the function of a leader is simply to convene. I say "simply" convene, but as should be obvious from this book, convening is neither simple nor easy when it comes to issues that really matter.

Some days are harder than others. I recall facilitating a critical decision meeting with 24 senior company leaders who had gathered from around the United States and Asia. The meeting lasted for nearly ten hours because the group felt it could not disband without a clear direction that every member would actively support. During the course of the deliberation, needs were clarified, shared goals identified, and hidden agendas uncovered. At

the conclusion of the meeting people were exhausted but satisfied with the realization that they had created much more than
just a policy decision. The consensus process transformed those
leaders' relationships with the company and with each other. It
created a level of directness and collaboration that set the stage
for a corporate-wide revitalization effort. During the course of
facilitating that meeting I felt as if I were standing in a hurricane
of complex issues and strong emotions. It was frightening, exhil-
arating, and exhausting—often at the same time. I share this
experience because I have no doubt you will one day find yourself in a similar situation. Storms are part of the natural land-
scape of participative decision making just as they are in nature.

In the "hurricane moments," I know it would be easy for me
to lose my footing. I can feel overwhelmed and anxious about my
ability to help the group come to a shared decision. I might feel
afraid of appearing incapable. I sometimes resent people in the
group because they are holding out for their preferred outcome. I
struggle against getting swept away by strong feelings others are
expressing, knowing that it's my job to be the one person in the
room who does not get carried away in a moment of high emotion or exhaustion. When a group is relying on me to be the calm
in the midst of the storm, what can I depend on to keep myself
from getting blown over? What enables me to keep both my feet
on the ground, my head in the conversation, and my heart connected to the group? When the work is most difficult, I find
myself relying on three things: the principles of consensus, the
voices of teachers, and my personal purpose and values.

Return to the Roots of Consensus

A tree is as strong as its roots. Likewise, any consensus conversation is as robust as its members' commitment to the core beliefs
of consensus. It is usually not enough to review these concepts at
the outset of a consensus process. These beliefs (see page 5) are
not common in many organizational cultures and therefore must

be reviewed and discussed on a regular basis until they become part of the group's natural language and thinking. I find that when a group gets "stuck," it is often because group members have forgotten or become confused about the basic definitions or principles that guide consensus. Getting the discussion back on track is often as simple as saying something like: *"This seems like a good time to remind you what it means to reach a consensus decision. You haven't actually reached consensus until each of you can say, 'I believe that this is the best decision for the organization at this time and I will support its implementation.'"*

I also know that not every consensus decision process need necessarily result in a consensus decision. As a facilitator, I need to remember that I cannot will a group to consensus. Nor can I create the preconditions required to make consensus possible (see page 6). I recall after one lengthy meeting in which a group was unable to reach consensus, one participant said, "God couldn't have gotten us to consensus today." I sometimes have to remind myself where my role and talents begin and end.

Remember the Words of My Teachers

With age I have come to draw more frequently from the people who have taught me important lessons that stay with me in the most challenging of times. Here are some of the lessons that calm, inspire, and guide me when I feel challenged during a consensus-building process.

When I am getting swept away in the drama of the moment, I remember William Ury's words, "Go to the balcony." In *Getting Past No: Negotiating Your Way from Confrontation to Cooperation* (New York: Bantam Books, 1991), Ury explains that the balcony is a metaphor for a mind-set of emotional detachment. It involves staying focused on what you are really trying to achieve, while at the same time distancing yourself from the very natural reactions that arise in the heat of conflict.

When I'm feeling pressure from myself or the group to make the process go faster, I remind myself to slow down. Peter Block taught me this. In his book *The Answer to How Is Yes: Acting on What Matters* (San Francisco: Berrett-Koehler, 2002), Block advises, "At times the only goal is to go faster. Acting on what matters means knowing that difference between moving quickly and knowing where we are going. . . . If we yield to the temptation of speed, we short-circuit our strategies and models into the world" (p. 79).

When I notice myself designing processes that are too complicated, Margaret Wheatley reminds me about the value of simplicity in *Turning to One Another: Simple Conversations to Restore Hope to the Future* (San Francisco: Berrett-Koehler, 2002): "I've seen myself pull back from simple more than once because I realized I wouldn't be needed any longer. Those are useful moments that force me to clarify what's more important—my expert status or making sure the work gets done well" (p. 20).

When I lose perspective and am certain that my public "failure" will be as painful as death itself, I turn to Woody Allen's observation in the movie *Love and Death* (1975), "There are worse things in life than death. Have you ever spent an evening with an insurance salesman?" Consensus is often used in the context of serious issues and high-stakes decisions. But just because issues are serious, it doesn't mean we can't approach them with playfulness and humor. I encourage you to find ways to model this in your work with groups.

Finally, when I search my mind and can't find a teacher that answers my burning question or addresses my deepest fear, I can always use a principle taught to me by Susan Scott: "Obey your instincts" (*Fierce Conversations: Achieving Success at Work and in Life, One Conversation at a Time*; New York: Penguin, 2002, p. 165). When it feels most risky, I encourage you to listen to your own judgment and accumulated wisdom. It will pay off.

Reconnect with My Purpose and Values

This book is about knowledge, skill, and method. So the last thing I want to do is belittle the notion of competence. Competence is important. However, I have seen many competent facilitators fail with groups because they were not authentic, transparent, or grounded in what they were there to contribute. They had what some might call "personal agendas." They wanted to be seen as an expert. They wanted to be liked by the group. They needed to be needed. In the most difficult moments, those types of agendas will defeat you and, more importantly, risk the success of the process.

I have a personal ritual before I facilitate any meeting, regardless of how difficult I expect the meeting to be. I answer three questions for myself, and I say the answers out loud. This works really well when I'm alone in a hotel room but can create some awkward moments if I am forced to do it in a plane or at Starbucks during final preparation. Those questions are:

- What am I here to contribute to this group? (And, what am I not here to contribute?)
- What is my real motivation for doing this work with this group? (And, what motives cannot enter the room with me?)
- What are the uncompromised beliefs about people, my work, and the value of consensus decision making that will ground me today—especially if things get tough?

The answers to these questions have evolved for me over the years as they will for you. I don't believe that there are right answers, only honest ones. And in coming to the honest answers, you may decide that you are not the right person to be working in a group consensus process. That is okay. Not everyone is.

In the preceding chapters I've used the commonly accepted language of "building" consensus. But in my experience, consensus is more like *sculpting*. We begin with the raw materials of facts, beliefs, and positions that at early stages in the conversation may seem unmalleable. Skillful dialogue, listening, acknowledging, and asking are the tools that soften people's positions and enable them to creatively blend their ideas. Consensus is at its best when we combine different, even conflicting, ideas to create something entirely original and truly responsive to the problem we are trying to solve.

I have frequently heard leaders wax poetic over their disappointments in people. They wish for employees who would take more initiative in their work. They long for citizens who care more about what's happening in their community. They ask where they can find organizational members who want to be more involved. What I hear these leaders asking for are people who are engaged and invested—body, mind, and heart. I call this a state of high commitment. It's not something that just happens. People commit to and passionately pursue the futures they have helped to shape. I do not believe complacency and resistance are the natural state of being for most of us. We want to commit to something. We want to have meaningful discussions about the things that really matter to us. We have a deep desire to search out and find the most creative and effective solutions to our most pressing problems. We want to express our beliefs and convictions with the reassurance that we won't be attacked, shunned, or otherwise judged for them. We want to influence—to be seen and to be heard.

This sculpting process is truly a craft. As such, it's not useful to be too attached to outcomes when you are learning the craft. There will be less-than-perfect moments of facilitation, ungraceful interventions, and groups that don't or won't reach consensus. There will also be wonderfully satisfying moments in which you assist a group in breaking through an impasse and finding a "third way." As with any craft, the mastery lies in the doing and not the outcomes. Each conversation holds a new challenge and a new lesson to be learned. Be alert to these lessons, stay present, and hone your craft.

When you bring a powerful method like consensus into a group and use it effectively, you awaken something that has probably been there all along: People express their best thinking, their deeply held convictions, and their highest hopes for what their organization or community can become. You also create an opportunity for people to discover and strengthen the connections between ideas and each other. And in today's world, those connections may be more valuable, more sustainable, and more transformative than the particular decision they made.

RESOURCE GUIDE

Books

Atlee, Tom, and Rosa Zubizaretta. *The Tao of Democracy: Using Co-Intelligence to Create a World That Works for All.* North Charleston, SC: Writers' Collective, 2003.

Avery, Michel, Barbara Strivel, Brian Auvine, and Lonnie Weiss. *Building United Judgment: A Handbook for Consensus Decision Making.* Madison, WI: Center for Conflict Resolution, 1999.

Bens, Ingrid. *Advanced Facilitation Strategies: Tools and Techniques to Master Difficult Situations.* San Francisco: Jossey Bass, 2005.

Block, Peter. *The Answer to How is Yes: Acting on What Matters.* San Francisco: Berrett-Koehler Publishers, 2002.

Doyle, Michael, and David Strauss. *How to Make Meetings Work.* San Francisco: Jove Publications, 1985.

Holman, Peg, Tom Devane, and Steve Cady. *The Change Handbook: Group Methods for Shaping the Future,* 2nd ed. San Francisco: Berrett-Koehler Publishers, 2006.

Isaacs, William. *Dialogue: The Art of Thinking Together.* New York: Doubleday, 1999.

Kahane, Adam. *Solving Tough Problems: An Open Way of Talking, Listening, and Creating New Realities.* San Francisco: Berrett-Koehler Publishers, 2004.

Kaner, Sam, with Lenny Lind, Catherine Toldi, Sarah Fisk, and Duane Berger. *Facilitator's Guide to Participatory Decision-Making.* Philadelphia: New Society Publishers, 1996.

Saint, Steven, and James R. Lawson. *Rules for Reaching Consensus: A Modern Approach to Decision Making.* San Francisco: Pfeiffer & Company, 1994.

Schwartz, Roger, Anne Davidson, Peg Carlson, and Sue McKinney. *The Skilled Facilitator Fieldbook : Tips, Tools, and Tested Methods for Consultants, Facilitators, Managers, Trainers, and Coaches.* San Francisco: Jossey Bass, 2005.

Scott, Susan. *Fierce Conversations: Achieving Success at Work and in Life, One Conversation at a Time.* New York: Penguin, 2002.

Susskind, L.S., S. McKearnan, and J. Thomas-Larmer, eds. *The Consensus Building Handbook: A Comprehensive Guide to Reaching Agreement.* Thousand Oaks, CA: Sage Publications, 1999.

Ury, William. *Getting Past No: Negotiating Your Way from Confrontation to Cooperation.* New York: Bantam Books, 1991.

Vogt, Eric E., Juanita Brown, and David Isaacs. *The Art of the Powerful Question: Catalyzing Insight, Innovation, and Action.* Mill Valley, CA: Whole Systems Associates, 2003.

Vroom, Victor, and Philip Yetton. *Leadership and Decision Making.* Pittsburgh: University of Pittsburgh Press, 1976.

Wheatley, Margaret. *Turning to One Another: Simple Conversations to Restore Hope to the Future.* San Francisco: Berrett-Koehler Publishers, 2002.

Videos

Consensus Decision-Making. Earlham College, Richmond, IN: Quaker Foundation of Leadership, 1987.

Twelve Angry Men. Dir. Sidney Lumet. MGM Studios. 1957. (Available through Amazon.com and most local video rental stores)

The Abilene Paradox: The Management of Agreement. CRM
Learning. 1999. (Available through www.crmlearning.com)

Lessons from the New Workplace. CRM Learning. 2002.
(Available through www.crmlearning.com)

Process Tools

Consensus Cards,™ a tool for high-quality decisions and
accelerated deliberations. *www.consensustools.com*

VIA3 Assured Collaboration is a web-based service that
combines audio, video, instant messaging, and real-time
information in one desktop application. *www.viack.com*

Organizations

Center for Collaborative Organizations   Formerly The Center
for the Study of Work Teams, it is based at the University of
North Texas and was created for the purpose of education and
research in all areas of collaborative work systems. *www.work-
teams.unt.edu*

Co-Intelligence Institute   CII promotes awareness of co-intelligence, the ability to wisely organize our lives together, with the
idea that all of us are wiser together than any of us could be
alone. It disseminates tools and ideas that can be applied to democratic renewal, community problems, organizational transfor-
mation, national and global crises, and the creation of just,
vibrant, sustainable cultures. www.co-intelligence.org

Greenleaf Center for Servant Leadership   The Center's mission
is to improve the caring and quality of all institutions through a

new approach to leadership, structure, and shared decision-making. *www.greenleaf.org*

International Association of Facilitators   IAF is a professional association that promotes, supports, and advances the art and practice of facilitation through methods exchange, professional growth, practical research, collegial networking, and support services. *www.iaf-world.org*

National Coalition for Dialogue and Deliberation   NCDD's mission is to bring together and support people, organizations, and resources in ways that expand the power of discussion to benefit society. *www.thataway.org*

Public Conversation Project   PCP helps people with fundamental disagreements over divisive issues develop the mutual understanding and trust essential for strong communities and positive action. *www.publicconversations.org*

Society for Organizational Learning   Created by Peter Senge and other thought leaders, SOL's purpose is to discover, integrate, and implement innovative theories and practices relative to organizational learning. *www.solonline.com*

INDEX

ABOUT THE AUTHOR

For more than fifteen years, Larry Dressler has designed and facilitated conversations and learning experiences that elicit new insights and inspire action in organizations. He is sought out by executive leaders as a trusted advisor on how to weave candor, commitment, collaboration and continuous learning into the fabric of the workplace.

As the founder of Blue Wing Consulting, Larry has traveled throughout the country speaking, consulting, and connecting with people who embody what he calls "Wide-Awake Leadership™." He has worked with a wide variety of organizations, including Nissan Motors, USC University Hospital, Starbucks, Washington Department of Ecology, Pediatric AIDS Foundation, U.S. Federal Protective Services, and Cisco Systems.

Described by clients as a "gentle instigator of breakthrough conversations," Larry's work has brought him to interesting places including the headquarters of companies in 30 industries, a "circus school" in Colorado, the Ecuadorian Amazon, and Skid Row, Los Angeles. Whether in a corporate boardroom, on a factory floor or underneath a rainforest canopy, Larry's special talent for posing powerful questions and setting collaboration in motion is at the heart of his work.

Larry's education combines the disciplines of social psychology and business strategy. He earned his BA degree in Sociology from UCLA and an MBA from the UCLA Anderson Graduate School of Management. He has also completed post-graduate coursework in Organizational Psychology. He lives with his wife, Linda in Boulder, Colorado.

BLUE WING CONSULTING, LLC

Blue Wing Consulting designs and facilitates breakthrough conversations and learning experiences for organizations that want to create change. Clients work with Blue Wing in the following ways:

> Setting strategic direction ★ Putting core values into practice ★ Building collaboration and teamwork ★ Making high-stakes decisions ★ Developing excellent leaders ★ Becoming environmentally and socially responsible ★ Creating an energizing, inspiring workplace

Contact information:
Tel: 303 440-0425
Email: info@bluewingconsulting.com
www.bluewingconsulting.com

CONSENSUSTOOLS.COM

Consensustools.com provides resources for people who want to bring consensus decision-making to their organizations and communities. Reusable *Consensus Cards*™ made from durable green, yellow and red credit card plastic are available on the site as well as useful articles, facilitator lists, and organizational links. *www.consensustools.com*

About Berrett-Koehler Publishers

Berrett-Koehler is an independent publisher dedicated to an ambitious mission: Creating a World that Works for All.

We believe that to truly create a better world, action is needed at all levels—individual, organizational, and societal. At the individual level, our publications help people align their lives with their values and with their aspirations for a better world. At the organizational level, our publications promote progressive leadership and management practices, socially responsible approaches to business, and humane and effective organizations. At the societal level, our publications advance social and economic justice, shared prosperity, sustainability, and new solutions to national and global issues.

A major theme of our publications is "Opening Up New Space." They challenge conventional thinking, introduce new ideas, and foster positive change. Their common quest is changing the underlying beliefs, mindsets, institutions, and structures that keep generating the same cycles of problems, no matter who our leaders are or what improvement programs we adopt.

We strive to practice what we preach—to operate our publishing company in line with the ideas in our books. At the core of our approach is *stewardship*, which we define as a deep sense of responsibility to administer the company for the benefit of all of our "stakeholder" groups: authors, customers, employees, investors, service providers, and the communities and environment around us.

We are grateful to the thousands of readers, authors, and other friends of the company who consider themselves to be part of the "BK Community." We hope that you, too, will join us in our mission.

BE CONNECTED

Visit Our Website

Go to www.bkconnection.com to read exclusive previews and excerpts of new books, find detailed information on all Berrett-Koehler titles and authors, browse subject-area libraries of books, and get special discounts.

Subscribe to Our Free E-Newsletter

Be the first to hear about new publications, special discount offers, exclusive articles, news about bestsellers, and more! Get on the list for our free e-newsletter by going to www.bkconnection.com.

Participate in the Discussion

To see what others are saying about our books and post your own thoughts, check out our blogs at www.bkblogs.com.

Get Quantity Discounts

Berrett-Koehler books are available at quantity discounts for orders of ten or more copies. Please call us toll-free at (800) 929-2929 or email us at bkp.orders@aidcvt.com.

Host a Reading Group

For tips on how to form and carry on a book reading group in your workplace or community, see our website at www.bkconnection.com.

Join the BK Community

Thousands of readers of our books have become part of the "BK Community" by participating in events featuring our authors, reviewing draft manuscripts of forthcoming books, spreading the word about their favorite books, and supporting our publishing program in other ways. If you would like to join the BK Community, please contact us at bkcommunity@bkpub.com.